Level 4: 1000 vocabulary words

Bad Luck Guy's Sea Adventures

倒霉蛋航海奇遇记

王帅 改编

MP3
Download Online
www.sinolingua.com.cn

First Edition 2016

ISBN 978-7-5138-1039-5
Copyright 2016 by Sinolingua Co., Ltd
Published by Sinolingua Co., Ltd
24 Baiwanzhuang Road, Beijing 100037, China
Tel: (86) 10-68320585 68997826
Fax: (86) 10-68997826 68326333
http://www.sinolingua.com.cn
E-mail: hyjx@sinolingua.com.cn
Facebook: www.facebook.com/sinolingua
Printed by Beijing Jinghua Hucais Printing Co., Ltd

Printed in the People's Republic of China

编者的话

对于广大汉语学习者来说，要想快速提高汉语水平，扩大阅读量是很有必要的。"彩虹桥"汉语分级读物为汉语学习者提供了一系列有趣、有用的汉语阅读材料。本系列读物按照词汇量进行分级，并通过精彩的故事叙述，给读者带来了丰富有趣的阅读享受。本套读物主要有以下特点：

一、分级精准，循序渐进。我们参考了新汉语水平考试（HSK）词汇表（2012年修订版）、《汉语国际教育用音节汉字词汇等级划分（国家标准）》和《常用汉语1500高频词语表》等词汇分级标准，结合《欧洲语言教学与评估框架性共同标准》（CEFR），设计了一套适合汉语学习者的"彩虹桥"词汇分级标准。本系列读物分为7个级别（入门级*、1级、2级、3级、4级、5级、6级），供不同水平的汉语学习者选择，每个级别故事的生词数量不超过本级别对应词汇量的20%。随着级别的升高，故事的篇幅逐渐加长。本系列读物与HSK、CEFR的对应级别，各级词汇量以及每本书的字数详见下表。

---

* 入门级（Starter）在封底用S标识。

级别	入门级	1级	2级	3级	4级	5级	6级
对应级别	HSK1 CEFR A1	HSK1-2 CEFR A1-A2	HSK2-3 CEFR A2-B1	HSK3 CEFR A2-B1	HSK3-4 CEFR B1	HSK4 CEFR B1-B2	HSK5 CEFR B2-C1
词汇量	150	300	500	750	1 000	1 500	2 500
字数	1 000	2 500	5 000	7 500	10 000	15 000	25 000

二、故事精彩，题材多样。本套读物选材的标准就是"精彩"，所选的故事要么曲折离奇，要么感人至深，对读者构成奇妙的吸引力。选题广泛取材于中国的神话传说、民间故事、文学名著、名人传记和历史故事等，让汉语学习者在阅读中潜移默化地了解中国的文化和历史。

三、结构合理，实用性强。"彩虹桥"系列读物的每一本书中，除了中文故事正文之外，都配有主要人物的中英文介绍、生词英文注释及例句、故事正文的英文翻译、练习题以及生词表，方便读者阅读和理解故事内容，提升汉语阅读能力。练习题主要采用客观题，题型多样，难度适中，并附有参考答案，既可供汉语教师在课堂上教学使用，又可供汉语学习者进行自我水平检测。

如果您对本系列读物有什么想法，比如推荐精彩故事、提出改进意见等，请发邮件到 liuxiaolin@sinolingua.com.cn，与我们交流探讨。也可以关注我们的微信公众号 CHQRainbowBridge，随时与我们交流互动。同时，微信公众号会不定期发布有关"彩虹桥"的出版信息，以及汉语阅读、中国文化小知识等。

韩 颖 刘小琳

Preface

For students who study Chinese as a foreign language, it's crucial for them to enlarge the scope of their reading to improve their comprehension skills. The "Rainbow Bridge" Graded Chinese Reader series is designed to provide a collection of interesting and useful Chinese reading materials. This series grades each volume by its vocabulary level and brings the learners into every scene through vivid storytelling. The series has the following features:

I. A gradual approach by grading the volumes based on vocabulary levels. We have consulted the New HSK Vocabulary (2012 Revised Edition), the *Graded Chinese Syllables, Characters and Words for the Application of Teaching Chinese to the Speakers of Other Languages (National Standard)* and the 1500 Commonly Used High Frequency Chinese Vocabulary, along with the Common European Framework of Reference for Languages (CEFR) to design the "Rainbow Bridge" vocabulary grading standard. The series is divided into seven levels (Starter*, Level 1, Level 2, Level 3, Level 4, Level 5 and Level 6) for students at different stages in their Chinese education to choose from. For each level, new words are no more than 20% of the vocabulary amount as specified in the corresponding HSK and CEFR levels. As the levels progress, the passage length will in turn increase. The following table indicates the corresponding "Rainbow Bridge" level, HSK and CEFR levels, the vocabulary amount, and number of characters.

---

* Represented by "S" on the back cover.

Level	Starter	1	2	3	4	5	6
HSK/ CEFR Level	HSK1 CEFR A1	HSK1-2 CEFR A1-A2	HSK2-3 CEFR A2-B1	HSK3 CEFR A2-B1	HSK3-4 CEFR B1	HSK4 CEFR B1-B2	HSK5 CEFR B2-C1
Vocabulary	150	300	500	750	1000	1500	2500
Characters	1000	2500	5000	7500	10,000	15,000	25,000

II. Intriguing stories on various themes. The series features engaging stories known for their twists and turns as well as deeply touching plots. The readers will find it a joyful experience to read the stories. The topics are selected from Chinese mythology, legends, folklore, literary classics, biographies of renowned people and historical tales. Such widely ranged topics would exert an invisible, yet formative, influence on readers' understanding of Chinese culture and history.

III. Reasonably structured and easy to use. For each volume of the "Rainbow Bridge" series, apart from a Chinese story, we also provide an introduction to the main characters in Chinese and English, new words with English explanations and sample sentences, and an English translation of the story, followed by comprehension exercises and a vocabulary list to help users read and understand the story and improve their Chinese reading skills. The exercises are mainly presented as objective questions that take on various forms with moderate difficulty. Moreover, keys to the exercises are also provided. The series can be used by teachers in class or by students for self-study.

If you have any questions, comments or suggestions about the series, please email us at liuxiaolin@sinolingua.com.cn. You can also exchange ideas with us via our WeChat account: CHQRainbowBridge. This account will provide updates on the series along with Chinese reading materials and cultural tips.

Han Ying and Liu Xiaolin

目 录
Contents

一、"倒霉蛋"文若虚……………………1

二、路遇洞庭红…………………………9

三、吉零国奇遇…………………………14

四、岛上捡到大龟壳……………………22

五、波斯商人玛宝哈……………………28

六、龟壳成了宝物………………………35

七、大龟壳的秘密………………………47

English Version ………………………51

练习题……………………………………69

练习题答案………………………………74

词汇表……………………………………75

主要人物和地点
Main Characters and Places

文若虚 (Wén Ruòxū)：一个读书人，经常遇到倒霉事，人称"倒霉蛋"。

Wen Ruoxu: A young intellectual who often encountered bad luck, hence the nickname "bad luck guy".

玛宝哈 (Mǎbǎohā)：波斯商人，专门和海外商人兑换珍宝货物。

Marboh: A Persian merchant who often exchanged treasures and other commodities with overseas businessmen.

张乘运 (Zhāng Chéngyùn)：专门出海做生意的商人，文若虚的好朋友。

Zhang Chengyun: A merchant who often went overseas to conduct business. He was a good friend of Wen Ruoxu.

苏州 (Sūzhōu)：江苏省的一个大城市。
Suzhou: A large city in Jiangsu Province.

北京 (Běijīng)：明朝时的首都，也就是现在的北京。
Beijing: Capital of the Ming Dynasty, the current Beijing.

泉州 (Quánzhōu)：福建省的城市，是很大的港口，有很多外国商人。

Quanzhou: A large port city in Fujian Province, which has gathered many foreign merchants.

吉零国 (Jílíngguó)：海外的一个国家。
Chi Ling State: An ancient overseas country.

波斯 (Bōsī)：海外的一个国家，一般认为是今天的伊朗。

Persia: An ancient overseas country, generally believed as present-day Iran.

中文故事

倒霉蛋航海奇遇记

一、"倒霉蛋①"文若虚

这个故事发生在中国的明朝②。苏州有一个年轻人,名叫文若虚,他从小就很聪明,学什么都很快,不管是读书、画画儿,还是弹琴③、下棋④,都十分精通⑤。他父亲是一个商人⑥,比较有钱,所以他从来没

---

① **倒霉蛋** (dǎoméidàn) n. bad luck guy
e.g., 他是一个倒霉蛋,做什么事都不成功。

② **明朝** (Míngcháo) n. Ming Dynasty (1368-1644)
e.g., 明朝是古代的一个朝代。

③ **弹琴** (tánqín) v. play the *guqin* or piano
e.g., 他没事的时候会弹弹琴,唱唱歌。

④ **下棋** (xiàqí) v. play chess
e.g., 他从小就喜欢下棋。

⑤ **精通** (jīngtōng) v. master, be well-versed in
e.g., 他从小就学习下棋,非常精通。

⑥ **商人** (shāngrén) n. businessman, merchant
e.g., 他是个商人,经常要去别的城市。

有为钱担心过,生活得很幸福。

当文若虚十几岁的时候,父亲把他叫到身边①,说:"儿子,你也不小了,要好好读书,准备参加科举②考试。"那时候只有经过科举考试才能当官③。文若虚很听话,开始准备科举考试。同学们都觉得他最聪明,成绩也好,肯定能考上。可是他考了好几次,他身边的同学几乎都

① 身边 (shēnbiān) n. one's side
e.g., 一辆车停在他的身边。

② 科举 (kējǔ) n. imperial examination, a civil service examination system in imperial China to select candidates for the state bureaucracy
e.g., 中国古代用科举考试选拔人才。

③ 当官 (dāngguān) v. become an official, reach officialdom
e.g., 很多人参加科举考试是为了当官。

① 安慰 (ānwèi) v.
console, comfort
e.g., 他很难过，需要别人安慰。

② 媒人 (méiren) n.
matchmaker
e.g., 她是我们两个人的媒人。

③ 说媒 (shuōméi) v.
act as a matchmaker
e.g., 她经常为别人说媒。

④ 新娘 (xīnniáng) n.
bride
e.g., 她明天就要结婚，成为新娘了。

⑤ 婚礼 (hūnlǐ) n.
wedding ceremony
e.g., 很多朋友都来参加他的婚礼。

⑥ 传来 (chuánlái) v.
pass, transmit
e.g., 外面传来了哭声。

⑦ 去世 (qùshì) v.
pass away
e.g., 他的父亲去年去世了。

⑧ 简直 (jiǎnzhí) adv.
simply
e.g., 他简直不敢相信自己的眼睛。

考上了，文若虚还是没考上。"我怎么这么倒霉呢？也许我不适合读书吧，还是干点别的吧。"文若虚这样安慰①自己。

这时有媒人②来给文若虚说媒③，文若虚的父母很高兴，就把结婚日期定了下来。听说新娘④很漂亮，文若虚也很高兴，每天忙着准备自己的婚礼⑤。可是到了结婚的前一天传来⑥消息，新娘突然去世⑦了。听到这个消息，文若虚简直⑧不敢相信自己的耳朵，"为什么我这么倒霉？还没结婚妻子就死了。"

没想到更倒霉的事还在后边。因为儿子考试和结婚的事,<u>文若虚</u>的父母受了很大的打击①,不久以后就双双去世了。<u>文若虚</u>伤心了几个月,人也越来越瘦。他的朋友担心他太难过,来安慰他说:"不能天天难过,生活还得继续。我看你学着做生意吧。听说咱们<u>苏州</u>的扇子②在北京很受欢迎,你买一些扇子

① 打击 (dǎjī) v.
blow, hit
e.g., 他考得这么差,你就别再打击他了。

② 扇子 (shànzi) n.
fan
e.g., 他在苏州买了一把扇子。

① 自从 (zìcóng) prep.
ever since
e.g., 自从工作以后，他的身体越来越不好。

② 装 (zhuāng) v.
pack, fill
e.g., 他的书包里装了很多书。

③ 箱子 (xiāngzi) n.
box, trunk
e.g., 这个箱子里装了很多东西。

到北京去卖，一定会赚很多钱的。"

文若虚也知道，自从①父母去世以后，家里剩下的钱已经不多了，所以他决定听从朋友的建议，去北京卖扇子。他从苏州买了几百把名人画的扇子，装②进箱子③带到北京去卖。"如果顺利的话，这一趟算起来能赚很多钱，"文若虚心里想，"希望这次我不会那么倒霉。"

文若虚到北京的时候是七月份。一般来说，七月份是北京最热的时候，扇子应该很好卖。可是文若虚到了北京，却发现这一年夏天一点也不热，而且从他到北京的第二天就开始下起大雨，几天都不停。文若虚非常着急，"怎么办呢？雨不停我也没办法去卖扇子呀。"

文若虚天天盼着①雨停下来。雨一连下了七天，这一天，雨终于停了，太阳出来了。文若虚终于松②了一口气："太好了！我终于可以去卖扇子了，只要卖出去一半，我就不会

① 盼（着）[pàn(zhe)] v. look forward to
e.g., 他盼着自己的孩子快点长大。

② 松 (sōng) v. relieve, relax
e.g., 知道自己的孩子没事，他松了一口气。

③ 赔 (péi) v. lose money in business
e.g., 这次做生意赔了很多钱。

① 晒 (shài) v. dry in the sun
e.g., 洗完了衣服,需要晒一晒。

② 潮湿 (cháoshī) adj. wet, damp
e.g., 下雨以后,空气很潮湿。

③ 纸张 (zhǐzhāng) n. paper
e.g., 这本书的纸张非常好。

④ 粘 (zhān) v. stick, glue
e.g., 巧克力都粘在一起了。

⑤ 乱七八糟 (luànqībāzāo) idiom in an awful mess
e.g., 孩子的房间里乱七八糟。

赔①。"他打开箱子,想把扇子拿出来晒②一晒,可是扇子怎么也打不开。原来因为天天下雨,空气潮湿③,扇子的纸张④都粘⑤在一起了。文若虚把扇子打开之后,发现扇子上的画都已经乱七八糟⑥,看不出来是什么了。文若虚差点哭了,"这样的扇子怎么会有人买呢？"

文若虚把扇子收拾了一下，只找出来十来把还可以卖的。卖了这些扇子，只够他回家的路费①。在回家的路上，文若虚几乎想自杀②了，"老天啊！还有比我更倒霉的人吗？考试考不过，结婚新娘死，父母都去世，做生意又赔光了本钱。我到底做错了什么，为什么老天这么惩罚③我？"

回到苏州，大家听说了文若虚的倒霉事，于是都在背后叫他"倒霉蛋"文若虚。

① 路费 (lùfèi) n.
travel expense
e.g., 回家的路费很贵。

② 自杀 (zìshā) v.
commit suicide
e.g., 他非常难过，甚至想到了自杀。

③ 惩罚 (chéngfá) v.
punish
e.g., 他犯了很大的错误，受到了惩罚。

① 街 (jiē) *n.* street
e.g., 妈妈上街买东西去了。

② 问候 (wènhòu) *v.* extend greetings to
e.g., 他们俩好久没有见面了，见面时互相问候了一下。

二、路遇洞庭红

"倒霉蛋"文若虚把家里的钱赔光了，只能靠着朋友和亲戚帮忙才能生活下去。这天，文若虚在街①上遇到了一个叫张乘运的老朋友。两个人互相问候②了一下后，文若虚问："张大哥，这段时间你在忙什么呢？""我啊，最近在忙着做生意。我和一些朋友买了很多东西，准备坐船出国去卖。"张乘运回答。

　　文若虚一想："反正① 我在苏州也没有什么事做，还不如跟他们一起出海② 碰碰运气③。就算赚不了钱，也能散散心④。"他把自己的想法⑤ 告诉了张乘运。张乘运想也没想就答应⑥ 了："没问题，反正我们的船很大，你也准备些货物⑦，咱们一起出海去卖。"

　　文若虚谢了张乘运，回家准备去了。可是他在家找来找去，也才找到了一两⑧ 多银子⑨。"这么点钱，我能买点什么

① 反正 (fǎnzhèng) *adv.* since, now that
e.g., 反正明天也不上班，晚点睡觉也没有关系。

② 出海 (chūhǎi) *v.* travel overseas
e.g., 明朝时有很多人出海做生意。

③ 碰运气 (pèng yùnqi) try one's luck
e.g., 他在中国过得很不好，决定出国碰碰运气。

④ 散心 (sànxīn) *v.* relieve boredom
e.g., 他心情不太好，想去别的地方散散心。

⑤ 想法 (xiǎngfa) *n.* idea, thought
e.g., 他很聪明，有很多想法。

⑥ 答应 (dāying) *v.* agree, consent
e.g., 我请她帮一个忙，她马上答应了。

⑦ 货物 (huòwù) *n.* goods, commodity
e.g., 这些货物可以卖很多钱。

⑧ 两 (liǎng) *m.w.* tael, a unit of weight for silver and gold in ancient China. According to the Ming Dynasty standard, one tael equals approximately 37.3 grams.
e.g., 明朝一两银子可以买 190 公斤左右大米。

⑨ 银子 (yínzi) *n.* silver, a currency by weight in ancient China that took on the form of silver ingots
e.g., 一两银子大概重 37.3 克。

① 橘子 (júzi) *n.*
orange
e.g., 橘子是很多人喜欢的水果。

② 老板 (lǎobǎn) *n.*
stall owner, boss
e.g., 他是个大老板，有很多钱。

③ 熟 (shú) *adj.*
ripe, cooked
e.g., 米饭熟了。

呢？"文若虚拿着钱，在街上一边走一边想。走着走着，文若虚突然看到路边有卖橘子①的，奇怪的是，这些橘子都是绿色的，所以没有什么人买。

"老板②，这是什么橘子啊？"文若虚问。

"这个叫作洞庭红，特别好吃。"老板回答他。

"可是这些橘子都是绿的，是不是还没熟③？"文若虚接着问。

"这您就不懂了，别看现在橘子是绿的，有点酸，但过一段时间，它就会变得特别甜。现在我卖得很便宜，一两银子可以给您两筐①。"老板解释说。

文若虚想："我那一两银子也买不了什么，不如就买两筐橘子吧，就算卖不了钱也可以给大家在路上吃。"于是他买了两筐带到了船上。

到了船上，大家都纷纷②过来跟文若虚打招呼，也看看他买了什么货。打开筐一看，是两筐绿橘子。好多人就笑起来："文先生，你可真有意思，这么绿的橘子，怎么可能卖出去啊？"

① 筐 (kuāng) n.
basket
e.g., 他把自己的衣服放在一个筐里。

② 纷纷 (fēnfēn) adv.
one after another
e.g., 听说他卖的水果很好吃，大家纷纷来买。

① 难怪 (nánguài) adv. no wonder
e.g., 他每天都跟中国人练习口语，难怪他汉语说得这么好。

② 大海 (dàhǎi) n. sea
e.g., 大海里有很多鱼。

还有人小声说："难怪①大家都叫他'倒霉蛋'，这次肯定又得赔了。"听了大家的话，文若虚心里也有点不舒服，但是又想，反正又没花多少钱，就当出去散散心。

就这样，倒霉蛋文若虚坐着大船，进入无边的大海②。"前面有什么事在等着我？我的运气会好一点吗？"文若虚想着想着，慢慢睡着了。

三、<u>吉零国</u>奇遇

大船在海上走了五六天，也不知道走了多远。这一天，大船终于在一座城市旁边停了下来。<u>文若虚</u>站起来，看到这座城市城墙①高大，城里人来人往，非常热闹。<u>张乘运</u>走过来对<u>文若虚</u>说："这是<u>吉零国</u>的首都，我们要下船卖东西了。"接着大家都纷纷下船，带着自己的货物到城里去卖。

看到大家都去赚钱，<u>文若虚</u>想："唉，可惜我没有本钱，只带了两筐绿橘子。反正也没事，不如把橘子拿出来晒一晒。"于是他把两筐橘子搬到岸上，打开筐却看到一片红光，

① 城墙 (chéngqiáng)
n. city wall
e.g., 这个城市有很多古代的城墙。

① 围 (wéi) v.
surround, encircle
e.g., 听说他卖的橘子很好吃,很多人围了过来。

② 剥 (bāo) v.
peel a shell
e.g., 橘子要剥皮吃。

原来过了这么几天,绿色的橘子都变红了。从远处看,这两筐橘子红得像火一样,非常吸引人。

不一会儿,很多人就围①了过来。"老板,这是什么东西啊?这么好看。"有人问。原来这<u>吉零国</u>并不产橘子,所以很多人不认识这种水果。<u>文若虚</u>也不回答,他拿起一个橘子,剥②开就吃了。

"原来是吃的呀，味道怎么样？"周围的人越来越多，都很好奇①。

"多少钱一个？"有人开始问价格了。

文若虚不知道这个国家用什么钱，也不知道要卖多少钱一个，这时船上的一个水手在那里开玩笑说："一个钱一个。"那个问价格的人真的拿出来一个钱递②给文若虚："来一个尝尝。"文若虚接过钱，发现这个钱是银的，大概一两左右。文若虚高兴坏了，"我这两筐橘子才花了一两银子，这一个橘子就把本钱赚回来了。"

那人剥开橘子，香气立刻③散发④出来。"真是好

---

① 好奇 (hàoqí) *adj.*
curious
e.g., 他来到一个新的地方，什么都感到好奇。

② 递 (dì) *v.*
pass, hand over
e.g., 他递给我一本书。

③ 立刻 (lìkè) *adv.* immediately, right away
e.g., 听到这个消息，他立刻回家了。

④ 散发 (sànfā) *v.*
distribute, give out
e.g., 这个花园散发着香气。

① 主人 (zhǔren) *n.* master, host
e.g., 他是这座房子的主人。

② 忍不住 (rěnbuzhù) cannot help but
e.g., 听到这个消息，他忍不住哭了起来。

③ 赶紧 (gǎnjǐn) *adv.* quickly, immediately
e.g., 看到时间不多了，他赶紧把饭吃完。

④ 讨价还价 (tǎo jià huán jià) *idiom* bargain, haggle over the price
e.g., 来这里买东西不能讨价还价。

⑤ 喊 (hǎn) *v.* yell
e.g., 不知道他在大声喊什么，大家都回头看他。

东西啊！"他一边吃一边说，"我要再买十个，给我主人①送去。"

听到这话，大家都忍不住②了，纷纷拿钱来买洞庭红。这个买十个，那个买五个，一会儿就差不多卖完了一筐。有的人没带钱，十分后悔。

眼看快卖完了，<u>文若虚</u>赶紧③说："剩下的这些不卖了，我还要留着自己吃呢。"

买东西的人急了："怎么能不卖呢？我买两个，出四个钱行不行？"

大家正在讨价还价④，突然来了一个骑着高头大马的人，大喊⑤着："不要卖了！剩下的我都要了！"

大家抬头一看,原来是第一个买橘子的那个人。他跳下马,跑到文若虚面前,说:"卖橘子的,剩下的橘子我都要了,我家主人要买了送给国王①吃。"别人一听是送给国王的,就都不抢②了,在旁边等着看。文若虚也是个聪明人,心

① 国王 (guówáng) n. king
e.g., 他是这个国家的国王。

② 抢 (qiǎng) v. scramble for
e.g., 那个人卖的水果很便宜,大家都抢着去买。

① 数 (shǔ) v. count
e.g., 他数了数，房间里一共有十个人。

② 付 (fù) v. pay
e.g., 今天他付钱请大家吃饭。

想："既然是送给国王的，他一定给的钱更多。"于是他说："剩下这些本来不打算卖的，如果你要的话，得三个钱一个。"

"没问题！"那人也不还价，"你来数①数还有多少个。"文若虚数了数，一共有五十二个，那人付②了一百五十六个钱，拿着橘子高高兴兴地走了。

文若虚回到船上，把钱收在一起数了数，大概有一千个钱，也就是一千两银子。"没想到两筐橘子卖了一千两银子，我的本钱也只有一两银子，真是太好了！"文若虚高兴地想着。

天黑了，大家都回到

了船上。文若虚把自己卖橘子的事情告诉了大家,大家听了都非常吃惊。有人很后悔:"两筐橘子卖了一千两?早知道我也带些橘子来卖了。"也有人祝贺文若虚:"看来你的坏运气到头了,以后就都是好运气啦!"还有人对他说:

① 笔 (bǐ) *m.w.* sum
e.g., 这次做生意，他赚了一大笔钱。

② 多亏 (duōkuī) *v.* be owing to
e.g., 多亏了朋友帮忙，他才顺利回到了家。

③ 满足 (mǎnzú) *v.* be satisfied
e.g., 看到自己的孩子很幸福，他很满足。

"你应该把赚的钱用来买一些货物，然后回国去卖，这样就又能赚一大笔①钱了。"文若虚想了想，说："大家都叫我倒霉蛋，以前卖什么东西都会赔钱。这次多亏②了大家，没有本钱却赚了一千两银子。但我也不敢去想再赚更多的钱，能赚这一千两我已经很满足③了。"大家听文若虚这样说，都说："唉，有钱还不去赚，真是可惜啊！"

四、岛①上捡②到大龟壳

这一次来到吉零国，大家都赚了一笔钱。张乘运对大家说："这次做生意很顺利，大家都赚到了钱。现在大海上风平浪静③，我们要不要去更远的地方再去赚大钱呢？"大家都说："去！去！我们坐船继续前进！"就这样，大船继续前进，慢慢到了波斯国附近。

这一天，本来风平浪静的海面忽然刮起了大风，接着乌云密布④，一场大雨就要来了。张乘运怕有危险，赶紧让水手们把船停到附近的岛边。到了岛边，水手把船停住，一场大雨果然⑤下了起来。雨下了一会儿，天晴了，大家终于

---

① 岛 (dǎo) *n.* island
e.g., 这个岛上一个人都没有。

② 捡 (jiǎn) *v.* pick up
e.g., 我在地上捡到一块钱。

③ 风平浪静 (fēngpíng-làngjìng) *idiom* with gentle breeze and fine ripples, calm and tranquil
e.g., 今天天气很好，大海上风平浪静。

④ 乌云密布 (wūyún mìbù) cloud over, be clouded
e.g., 天空突然乌云密布，要下雨了。

⑤ 果然 (guǒrán) *adv.* really, as expected
e.g., 很多人说他不会来，结果他果然没来。

放了心。张乘运说:"我们就在这休息一下,明天再出发。"

文若虚在船上待①着无聊,想到岛上去看看。大家都说:"这岛上好像没人,怕有危险,还是别去了。"文若虚说:"大家放心,我走不远。"

文若虚来到岛上,发现到处是高高的大树,地

① 待 (dāi) v. stay
e.g., 外面下着雨,他待在家里很无聊。

上的草长得也有一人高。不远处有一座小山，看起来风景①很美。文若虚想："不如我去山顶②上看看风景吧。"好在这座山并不高，他很快爬③到了山顶。站在山顶，文若虚四处④看去，到处是绿油油⑤的一片，风景果然很美。

突然，他发现不远处有一个大东西，看起来像是一只乌龟⑥，但是怎么会

① 风景 (fēngjǐng) n. scenery, view
e.g., 这里的风景非常漂亮。

② 山顶 (shāndǐng) n. hilltop, top of a mountain
e.g., 到山顶的时候，大家都非常累。

③ 爬 (pá) v. climb, ascend
e.g., 他最喜欢爬山了。

④ 四处 (sìchù) n. everywhere, all round
e.g., 他遇到了麻烦，四处找人帮忙。

⑤ 绿油油 (lǜyóuyóu) adj. lush green
e.g., 春天的时候，到处都是绿油油的。

⑥ 乌龟 (wūguī) n. tortoise, turtle
e.g., 乌龟爬得很慢。

① 蹲 (dūn) v.
squat, crouch
e.g., 他蹲在地上，好像是肚子疼。

② 靠近 (kào jìn) v.
approach
e.g., 他一点一点向她靠近。

③ 巨大 (jù dà) adj.
huge, giant
e.g., 这是一个巨大的错误。

④ 壳 (ké) n. shell
e.g., 乌龟过一段时间就会换壳。

有这么大的乌龟呢，简直像一个小山包。文若虚心里一下子紧张起来："看来我的运气还是没有变好，这么大的乌龟，肯定会把我吃了的。"他刚想往船上跑，又怕这只大乌龟追上来，只好蹲①在那里仔细看这个可怕的大东西。等了一会，却发现这只大乌龟一动也不动。"难道是一只死乌龟？"文若虚慢慢靠近②它，这个大东西还是一动也不动。到了它的面前，文若虚才发现那个东西是一个巨大③的乌龟壳④。文若虚松了一口气："还好只是一个乌龟壳。看来这个岛上肯定有特别危险的动物，我还是赶紧回船上去吧。"

文若虚转身①要走,走了两步②,又想:"不如我把这个大龟壳带回去吧,这么大的乌龟肯定大家都没见过。到时候我还可以跟我的邻居吹吹牛③,让他们知道我在国外有多么奇特④的经历。"于是,文若虚拖⑤着大龟壳往船的方向走去。

① 转身 (zhuǎnshēn) v. turn around
e.g., 他看到自己的爸爸,转身就跑了。

② 步 (bù) n. step
e.g., 他走了几步就摔倒了。

③ 吹牛 (chuīniú) v. brag, talk big
e.g., 这个人特别喜欢吹牛,大家都不喜欢他。

④ 奇特 (qítè) adj. peculiar, extraordinary
e.g., 他常常有奇特的想法,跟别人都不一样。

⑤ 拖 (tuō) v. drag, haul
e.g., 东西很重,他只能拖着走。

① 在意 (zàiyì) v.
mind, care about
e.g., 这次做生意赔了很多钱，但他却不在意。

② 干脆 (gāncuì) adv.
just, simply
e.g., 下雨了，咱们干脆别出去了。

回到船上，大家都围过来问："文先生，这是什么东西啊？"

"你们都买了那么多货，这个东西就是我的货。看，这么大的龟壳，你们没见过吧。"文若虚得意地说。

"这东西谁买呀？肯定卖不出去。"大家都笑话文若虚。

文若虚也不在意①，干脆②把大龟壳当作一个箱子，把自己的东西都放在里面。

五、波斯商人玛宝哈

第二天，风停了，张乘运对大家说："大家都买好了货，我们这就回国去吧。"大家都说好。于是，大船向泉州开去。那时候泉州是一个繁华①的港口②，来来往往的商人非常多。商人们从海外带着货物来到泉州，而泉州当地也有另外一些商人买这些

① 繁华 (fánhuá) adj. bustling, busy
e.g., 这是一个繁华的大城市。

② 港口 (gǎngkǒu) n. port, harbor
e.g., 港口停着许多船。

① 卸 (xiè) v.
discharge, unload
e.g., 港口边有很多人在那边卸货。

② 岸 (àn) n.
shore, bank
e.g., 船到了港口，大家都上岸了

③ 客商 (kèshāng) n.
traveling merchant
e.g., 各地的客商都来到这个港口做生意。

④ 值 (zhí) v. be worth
e.g., 这些货物值很多钱。

⑤ 饭店 (fàndiàn) n.
restaurant, hotel
e.g., 这家饭店的饭很好吃。

⑥ 招牌 (zhāopai) n.
signboard, shop sign
e.g., 这家饭店门口挂着很大的招牌。

货物，再把这些货物卖到全国各地。

这一天，文若虚坐的大船到了泉州，大家纷纷把货物卸①下船。文若虚只有一个大龟壳，所以也没着急把龟壳弄上岸②。这时候来了一个人对大家喊："各位客商③，我们的老板玛宝哈请大家吃饭。"

文若虚奇怪地问："张大哥，这玛宝哈是个什么样的人啊？"

张乘运介绍说："这个玛宝哈是泉州这里最出名的波斯商人，非常有钱，也特别有眼光，一眼就能看出你的货物值④多少钱。"

大家跟着那个人，来到了一个大饭店⑤，招牌⑥

上写着四个大字"同福饭店"。饭店门口站着一个高个子的外国人。张乘运小声对文若虚说:"这个人就是玛宝哈,大家都叫他玛老板。"文若虚抬头一看,发现这个玛宝哈长着蓝色的眼睛,高高的鼻子,留着大胡子①,穿的衣服倒是和中国人没什么区别。

① 胡子 (húzi) *n.* beard, mustache
e.g., 他的胡子很长。

① 熟 (shú) *adj.*
familiar
e.g., 他们俩很熟，是好朋友。

② 招呼 (zhāohu) *n.*
greeting
e.g., 他俩见面的时候，互相打了个招呼。

③ 称赞 (chēngzàn) *v.*
praise, commend
e.g., 老师称赞学生的作业写得很好。

④ 宝物 (bǎowù) *n.*
treasure
e.g., 这次出海做生意，他得到了一些宝物。

⑤ 价钱 (jiàqian) *n.*
price
e.g., 这件衣服的价钱很高。

⑥ 珍珠 (zhēnzhū) *n.*
pearl
e.g., 这些珍珠值很多钱。

⑦ 宝石 (bǎoshí) *n.*
gem, precious stone
e.g., 这些宝石非常漂亮，也很值钱。

看起来很多人都和玛宝哈很熟①，玛宝哈也热情地和商人们打着招呼②。"没想到这个波斯人汉语说得这么好！"文若虚在心里称赞③。

这时候玛宝哈大声对大家说："各位老朋友、新朋友！我是波斯商人玛宝哈，今天在同福饭店请大家喝酒，吃饭。大家这次带来了什么宝物④，都来让我看看，我出的价钱⑤一定是最高的。"于是大家一个个过来跟玛宝哈介绍自己进的货。这个说，"玛老板，这次我带了很多珍珠⑥"；那个说，"玛老板，这次我进了好多宝石⑦"……玛宝哈非常高兴，

让那些进了很多宝物的商人坐到旁边。

过了一会儿,玛宝哈走到了文若虚的面前,笑着说:"这位老板,你带了什么宝物啊?"文若虚什么货都没有进,不知道怎么回答,非常尴尬①。张乘运赶紧过来说:"玛老板,这是我的朋友,只是跟我们出海散散心的。"玛老板

① 尴尬 (gāngà) *adj.* embarrassed
e.g., 他们俩刚认识,不知道说什么,有点尴尬。

① 宴席 (yànxí) *n.*
banquet, feast
e.g., 宴席还没开始,先别吃。

② 讲究 (jiǎngjiu) *n.*
attention to detail, careful study
e.g., 喝茶很有讲究,不同的季节喝不同的茶。

③ 角落 (jiǎoluò) *n.*
corner, remote place
e.g., 他坐在房间的一个角落,很难看到他。

笑了一下,也不说话,转身问其他商人去了。

宴席①的座位安排得很有讲究②,谁带的宝物越多越值钱,谁的座位离玛宝哈就越近,那些带的货物少或者不值钱的,只能坐在后面。文若虚没有货物,自然坐在了一个没有人的角落③。

看着大家都在热闹地聊天，却没有人理①自己，文若虚心里有点难过："唉，虽然我这次赚了一千两银子，但和这些大商人比起来，真是不起眼呀！早知道我也买一些货物，至少可以不这么丢脸。"看着大家在旁边开心地聊天，喝酒，文若虚又想起了之前的倒霉事，心想："唉，反正也没人理我，我就自己喝酒吧。"不知不觉②，文若虚就喝醉③了，倒在了椅子上。

① 理 (lǐ) v. heed, pay attention to
e.g., 他生气了，不理我了。

② 不知不觉 (bùzhī-bùjué) idiom unknowingly, unconsciously
不知不觉孩子就长大了。

③ 醉 (zuì) v. be drunk
e.g., 他那天喝了很多酒，最后喝醉了。

六、龟壳成了宝物

第二天醒来,文若虚已经在床上了。他坐起来,觉得头有点疼,怎么也想不起来昨天是怎么回到船上的。忽然听到船外面声音很大,"玛老板来啦!""玛老板好!"原来是玛宝哈来船上看货了,大家都抢着给他介绍自己的货物。

"玛老板,这是我的宝石,您看看。"

"玛老板,这是我的珍珠,您瞧①瞧。"

玛宝哈一边客气地点点头,一边四处看看,好像对这些货物都不是特别满意。突然,他走到文若虚的"箱子"——大龟壳

---

① 瞧 (qiáo) v.
look, see
e.g., 你瞧,这是我新买的包,漂亮吧?

旁边，摸①了摸这个龟壳，激动地说："这是哪位老板的货？是要卖的吗？"

"那是<u>文若虚</u>的货。"大家看玛宝哈对这个龟壳感兴趣，都很奇怪。

"<u>文若虚</u>？昨天他参加我的宴会②了吗？"玛宝哈对这个名字一点印象都没有。

"去了呀，坐在最后面的位置③，后来喝醉了，现在就在船上。"大家提醒他。

"哎呀！我真是慢待④了贵客⑤，怎么能让<u>文先生</u>坐在最后面呢？快，让我再认识一下<u>文先生</u>！"玛宝哈急得不得了。

大家带着玛宝哈来到

① 摸 (mō) v.
touch, stroke
e.g., 妈妈摸着孩子的头。

② 宴会 (yànhuì) n.
banquet, feast
e.g., 明天请你来我家参加我的生日宴会。

③ 位置 (wèizhi) n.
position, seat
e.g., 这个位置很好，可以看得很清楚。

④ 慢待 (màndài) v.
treat a guest inadequately
e.g., 他慢待了客人，客人们也不太高兴。

⑤ 贵客 (guìkè) n.
distinguished guest
e.g., 家里来了贵客，我要好好接待。

① 鞠躬 (jūgōng) v.
bow
e.g., 他要离开的时候，给自己的老师鞠了一躬。

② 疯 (fēng) adj.
mad, crazy
e.g., 你疯了吧？这个不能吃！

文若虚面前，玛宝哈深深地鞠了一个躬①，说："文先生，昨天是我的不对，慢待了贵客。我现在马上重新举办一个宴会，专门请您，您一定要来！"

看到玛宝哈对文若虚这么礼貌，大家都很奇怪。有人说："这玛宝哈是不是疯②了，文若虚也没有什么货物，就这么一个龟壳，会那么值钱吗？"还有人说："谁知道呢，都说这个波斯人特别识货①，看来也没什么。"

文若虚看到昨天正眼也不看自己的玛宝哈突然对自己这么热情，也觉得很奇怪，想："既然他请我，我就去看看他想要什么。"

文若虚跟着玛宝哈来到同福饭店，店里已经摆②下了特别丰盛③的宴席，比昨天的宴席要高档④很多。玛宝哈让文若虚坐在最中间的位置，自己坐在旁边陪着他，而别的商人都坐在不重要的位置。

"文老板，"玛宝哈举起一杯酒说，"昨天我慢待您了，我郑重⑤向您道歉。

① 识货 (shíhuò) *v.*
be a knowledgeable buyer
e.g., 他不太识货，买了一些不值钱的东西。

② 摆 (bǎi) *v.*
serve, arrange
e.g., 他们摆了一桌宴席来迎接客人。

③ 丰盛 (fēngshèng)
adj. sumptuous, rich
e.g., 今天的宴席有很多菜，特别丰盛。

④ 高档 (gāodàng)
adj. luxurious, high-grade
e.g., 这件衣服很高档。

⑤ 郑重 (zhèngzhòng)
adj. serious, earnest
e.g., 知道自己错了，他郑重向老师道了歉。

① 尊贵 (zūnguì) *adj.* honorable, respected
e.g., 这位客人非常尊贵，每个人对他都特别客气。

② 疑问 (yíwèn) *n.* question
e.g., 很多事情都不明白，他心里有很多疑问。

③ 谦虚 (qiānxū) *adj.* modest
e.g., 虽然他很优秀，但也很谦虚。

我做生意几十年了，但您是我遇到的最尊贵①的客人。"说完，他一口把酒都喝了。

"哪里，哪里。其实我这次没买什么货，不知道玛老板为什么这么客气呢？"文若虚说出了心里的疑问②。

"文老板太谦虚③了。您的货我看过了，是我做生意这么多年以来，见到的最值钱的货！"玛宝哈笑着说。

"我真的没带什么货，玛老板是不是看错货了？"文若虚更觉得奇怪了。

"难道文先生不打算卖吗，您那件宝物大龟壳……"玛宝哈以为文若虚舍不得,有点着急了。

"哦,您是说那个龟壳呀。"文若虚这才明白玛宝哈是看中了他的大龟壳。"这个大龟壳值什么钱呢?"文若虚心里想,"不过从玛宝哈的态度来看,那是件宝物。我也不能表现①出我什么都不懂。"于是文若虚装②出很为难的样子,说:"玛老板,原来你是看中了我那件宝物呀。其实,那件宝物我打算自己收藏③,不想卖给别人。"

玛宝哈一听就急了:"哎,先生先不要一口拒绝,至少说个价格出来。"文若虚有点为难了,因为他确实不知道应该要多少钱。要多了,怕玛宝哈生

① 表现 (biǎoxiàn) v.
show, manifest
e.g., 他表现得很自信。

② 装 (zhuāng) v.
pretend
e.g., 孩子不想上学,故意装病。

③ 收藏 (shōucáng) v.
collect, store up
e.g., 他喜欢收藏各种书。

① **偷偷** (tōutōu) *adv.*
stealthily, secretly
e.g., 看到没人注意，他偷偷走了。

② **伸** (shēn) *v.* stretch out one's hand
e.g., 他伸出手和我握手。

③ **瞪** (dèng) *v.* open one's eyes wide
e.g., 他瞪大眼睛看着我，一句话也说不出来。

气；要少了，又怕大家笑话。于是回头看看张乘运，张乘运偷偷①给他伸②出了五个手指头。文若虚想："五千两银子，有点太多了吧，不管了，试试吧。"于是文若虚向玛宝哈伸出了五个手指。

"五万两银子？"玛宝哈瞪③大眼睛说。

文若虚只想要五千两,没想到玛宝哈以为是五万两,刚要解释,只见玛宝哈两眼放光,接着说:"先生当真吗?五万两可以卖给我?"文若虚有点糊涂①了,真不知道玛宝哈是嫌②贵还是嫌便宜,只能点点头。

"好!"玛宝哈激动地站起来,对大家说,"请各位老板做见证③,文先生愿意以五万两的价格把自己的宝物卖给我。"

大家一听大龟壳能卖五万两银子,都吃惊得张大了嘴。而看到玛宝哈一口答应给这么高的价钱,文若虚心想:"肯定是价钱要的低了。不过也不错,

① 糊涂 (hútu) *adj.* muddled, bewildered
e.g., 你太糊涂了,怎么能相信他的话呢?

② 嫌 (xián) *v.* dislike, complain of
e.g., 我嫌那件衣服太贵,就没买。

③ 见证 (jiànzhèng) *v.* witness
e.g., 很多人见证了这个重要的时刻。

① **富翁** (fùwēng) *n.* man of wealth
e.g., 他赚了一大笔钱，成了大富翁。

谁能想到一个捡来的大龟壳能卖五万两银子啊。这回我一下子就成大富翁①了！"所以文若虚也很高兴，答应把大龟壳卖给玛宝哈。

玛宝哈很着急，生怕文若虚后悔，说："文先生，既然您决定把您的宝物卖给我，请您先去把宝物拿过来吧。"于是，文若虚带着人到了船上，把大龟壳带回了同福饭店。

回到同福饭店以后，玛宝哈已经准备了好几个大箱子，里面全是白花花的银子。玛宝哈笑着说："文先生，这些银子都是您的了。不过这还不够五万两，我这里有几处房子，

还有这个<u>同福饭店</u>，还有我的这些<u>仆人</u>①，加在一起就差不多了，所以这一切都是您的了。"

<u>文若虚</u>一看，自己不仅有了这么多银子，还有了自己的房子和饭店，非常高兴，就正式把大龟壳给了<u>玛宝哈</u>。<u>玛宝哈</u>非常激动，叫人仔细收好。

① 仆人 (púrén) n. servant
e.g., 仆人要听主人的话。

① 转运 (zhuǎnyùn) v.
have a turn of luck
e.g., 人不会一直倒霉，总会转运的。

② 特地 (tèdì) adv.
specially
e.g., 他特地从外地回来参加这次宴席。

③ 发财 (fācái) v.
make a fortune
e.g., 他得到了一大笔钱，发了大财。

④ 心意 (xīnyì) n.
regard, kindly feeling
e.g., 东西不值钱，但是是我的心意。

文若虚一下子成了大富翁，心想："这下我真的是转运①了！"于是他站起来对一起出海的商人们说："我文若虚本来是一个倒霉蛋，做什么生意都赔钱，这次却做了这么大的生意，都是因为和大家一起出海，才有了我今天的转运。所以我决定送大家每人一百两银子，请大家收下。"

大家都非常高兴，收下了银子，纷纷感谢文若虚。文若虚又特地②来到张乘运面前，说："张大哥，这次我出海做生意，没想到能发财③。我能有今天，都是多亏了你啊！这是一千两银子，是我的心意④，请你收下。"张乘运说:"哎,哪里是我的功劳①?人不会一直都倒霉的,你的运气来了,怎么都能发财。恭喜②你啦!"说完他也把一千两收下,向文若虚表示感谢。

① 功劳 (gōngláo) n. contribution, credit
e.g., 这次我们能够成功,全是他的功劳。

② 恭喜 (gōngxǐ) v. congratulate
e.g., 听说你有了孙子,恭喜你!

① 秘密 (mìmì) n.
secret
e.g., 她的秘密从来不告诉别人。

② 告别 (gàobié) v.
bid farewell to
e.g., 他告别了父母，去外地工作了。

③ 财产 (cáichǎn) n.
wealth, possession
e.g., 他是个富翁，有很多财产。

七、大龟壳的秘密①

文若虚住进了玛宝哈的房子，一夜也没睡着。

第二天，玛宝哈前来告别②，说："文先生，我就要回波斯了，特地来向您告别。"文若虚说："玛老板在泉州这么多年，为什么决定回国了？"

玛宝哈笑着说："我在这里的财产③都转给您了。不过有那个大龟壳，等我回国以后把它卖掉，不光我，我的儿子、孙子都不用工作啦。"

文若虚说："玛老板，我一直有一个问题不明白，想向您请教。这个龟壳到底有什么特别的地方，为什么会这么值钱？"

玛宝哈大笑起来:"你们中国人都崇拜①龙②,怎么会不认识这个龟壳呢?"

"这个龟壳和龙有什么关系呢?"文若虚更奇怪了。

玛宝哈解释说:"传说每条龙都有九个孩子,每一个都不一样。其中有一个孩子叫鼍龙③,可以活一万岁。这鼍龙生下来就有壳,看起来就像乌龟一样。每过一百年,它就会脱一次壳。到一千岁时,它最后一次脱壳,然后就变成真正的龙飞走了。这时候它的壳里面就会有二十四颗④夜明珠⑤,这些夜明珠巨大无比,晚上拿出来可以照亮整个房间。你

① 崇拜 (chóngbài) v. worship, admire
e.g., 他唱歌唱得很好,很多人崇拜他。

② 龙 (lóng) n. dragon
e.g., 中国人认为自己是龙的传人。

③ 鼍龙 (tuólóng) n. a type of dragon in ancient Chinese mythology, which is also another name of the Chinese alligator
e.g., 鼍龙是龙的九子之一。

④ 颗 (kē) m.w. (for things small and roundish)
e.g., 这是一颗珍珠。

⑤ 夜明珠 (yèmíngzhū) n. legendary luminous pearl
e.g., 夜明珠可以把整个房间照亮。

① 珍贵 (zhēnguì) *adj.*
precious, valuable
e.g., 夜明珠是非常珍贵的宝物。

卖给我的龟壳，其实就是鼍龙最后一次脱下的壳，我已经把它打开，里面真的有二十四颗夜明珠。在我们国家，这些夜明珠每一颗都能卖五万两银子！"

文若虚听了玛宝哈的解释，吃惊得瞪大了眼睛，原来自己捡的龟壳居然是这么珍贵①的宝物。不过文

若虚也很高兴，因为要不是遇到知识丰富的玛宝哈，说不定自己现在还把龟壳当箱子呢。

从此以后，文若虚就在泉州住下来，过上了幸福的生活。而"倒霉蛋"成为"大富翁"的故事，一直传到了今天。

English Version

Bad Luck Guy's Sea Adventures

I. Wen Ruoxu, the "Bad Luck Guy"

This story occurred in the Ming Dynasty of China. In the city of Suzhou, there was a young man named Wen Ruoxu. He was very smart since childhood and was quick at learning everything. Wen was adept at reading, painting, playing the *guqin* and chess. His father was a rich merchant, so Wen never had money trouble and led a happy life.

When he became a teenager, his father called him over one day and said, "My son, since you have grown up, you should study hard and prepare for the imperial exams." Back then, taking the imperial examinations was the only path to office. Wen accepted his father's advice and began preparing for the exams. In the eyes of his classmates, he was the smartest among them and had the best test results, so they had no doubts that he would make it. Unfortunately, he failed several times, while almost all his classmates succeeded. "What bad luck I have! Perhaps I'm not suitable to be a scholar. I'd better try something else." He comforted himself.

One day, a matchmaker arrived at Wen's family to introduce him to a future wife. His parents were very glad and decided on a marriage date for the couple. Wen was also happy to hear the bride was very beautiful, and he was busy preparing for his wedding everyday. However, bad news came just one day before his big date: the bride passed way all of a sudden. Upon learning about the tragedy, Wen simply couldn't believe what he heard. "What a misfortune! My future wife died just before our wedding!"

It never occurred to the family that more bad luck was yet to come. Wen's failure on the exams and his unlucky marriage delivered a heavy blow to his parents, so much so that they both passed away right afterwards. He suffered from grief for several months and became thinner and thinner. One of his friends felt worried and tried to console him by saying, "You shouldn't throw yourself into sadness each and every day as life has to go on. I suggest you do some business because I heard that the fans produced here in Suzhou are very popular in Beijing. Go and buy some fans and sell them there, and I'm sure you will make a lot of money."

Wen was well aware that ever since his parents' death, there had been not much money left in the family. So he decided to take his friend's advice of going to Beijing to sell fans. He bought hundreds of fans with famous painting designs from Suzhou and packed them all into a trunk. "If everything goes well, I could earn a lot of money from this trip," he thought, "Hopefully bad luck will go away from me this time."

It was July when he arrived in Beijing. Generally, it's the hottest month, so fans should be easy to sell. Upon his arrival however, Wen found the summer that year was not hot at all. Even worse, it began raining heavily the next day and lasted several days. Wen worried a lot and thought, "What can I do? I can't sell the fans if the rain continues."

Everyday Wen was looking forward to a stop of the rain. After seven consecutive days it finally stopped and the sun came out. He heaved a sigh of relief and said, "This is awesome! Now I'm able to sell my fans. I won't suffer any losses as long as half of them could be sold." He opened the trunk to take the fans out and put them under the sun, but they couldn't be unfolded no matter how hard he tried. It turned out that the continuous rainfall had dampened the air so that the fan paper had all stuck together. Eventually he managed to unfold them, but discovered that the pictures had become blurred and beyond recognition. Wen almost cried, "Could there be anybody who wants to buy fans like these?"

He tidied up the fans and only found around ten of them that could still be sold. The money he received was just enough to cover his return trip. On his way back home, Wen was even thinking about death, "My goodness! Is there anyone who is more unlucky than I am? I flunked the exams, lost my bride before our wedding, my parents both died, and I lost all capital in my business... What did I do wrong? Why has God punished me like this?"

As Wen arrived back in Suzhou, people learned about his unfortunate experiences, then started calling him the "bad luck guy" behind his back.

Section 2 Encountering "Dongting Red"

Having lost all his family's wealth, Wen Ruoxu, the "bad luck guy", had to rely on the assistance of his friends and relatives for a living. One day, he met his old friend Zhang Chengyun by chance on the street. The two exchanged greetings as Wen asked Zhang, "Brother Zhang, what have you been busy with recently?" "Me? I've been engaged in my business. I bought a lot of stuff together with my friends and we are going to take a ship overseas and sell the goods." Zhang replied.

Wen thought, "Now that I don't have much to do here in Suzhou, why not travel overseas with them and try my luck? I may not be able to make any money, but at least it's a way to relieve my boredom." He then shared the idea with Zhang, who agreed without hesitation, "No problem. Since there is plenty room on our ship, you can prepare some goods as well and go with us to sell them."

Wen thanked Zhang and returned home to get everything prepared. After a long search in his house, he only found more than one tael of silver. "What can I purchase with such little money?" He pondered while walking on the street with the money. Suddenly he saw there was an orange stall on the roadside. Surprisingly, all of the oranges were green and as a result, there were few buyers.

"Excuse me, what kind of oranges are these?" Wen asked.

"These are called Dongting Red, which are quite tasty." The vendor answered.

"But all of them look green, are they not ripe yet?" Wen asked again.

"You may not know this, sir. Although the oranges are green and a bit sour now, they will become very sweet after a certain period of time. I'm selling them at a rather low price and you can get two baskets for just one tael of silver." The man explained.

Wen thought, "There are few things I can buy with the tael of silver I have, I may as well buy two baskets of oranges. Even though I couldn't make much money from them, I can share with others along the trip." He then bought the oranges and brought them onto the ship.

As Wen boarded the ship, people all came to greet him and take a look at the goods he bought. After the cover was lifted, two baskets of green oranges appeared. Many people laughed, "Mr. Wen, you are so interesting! How can green oranges be sold?" Someone else whispered, "No wonder people call him 'bad luck guy', he will surely lose money again this time!" Hearing what others said, Wen felt pretty sad. But after a second thought, "After all it didn't cost me much money, I may as well travel overseas to relax myself."

Thus our "bad luck guy" entered the vast sea onboard the large ship. "What is waiting for me ahead? Will my luck change?" Gradually he fell asleep.

Section 3 Adventures in the Chi Ling State

The ship had been traveling for five to six days at the sea and no one could tell how much distance was covered. One day, the crew anchored by a city. Wen stood up and saw abustling scene within the high city wall. Zhang Chengyun came over and said to him, "This is the capital of the Chi Ling State. We'll get off to sell our goods." People disembarked the ship one by one with their commodities and headed for the city.

Seeing that others had set off to earn money, Wen thought, "Alas! It's a pity that I don't have much capital. I only brought two baskets of oranges with me. Since I have nothing else to do now, why not place them under the sun to help them ripe?" So he carried the baskets onshore and opened them: a scene of redness came into view. In fact, after these few days, the green oranges had all turned into red. Seen from afar, the two baskets of oranges looked as red as fire, which was quite enticing.

Soon many people gathered around him. "Excuse me, what are these? They look so nice!" Someone asked. Actually, this place does not produce oranges, so many people didn't recognize them. Wen didn't give an answer but took up an orange, peeled and ate it.

"Oh, it's something to eat. How is the taste?" The curious crowd began to grow.

"How much does one cost?" Someone began to ask for price.

Wen knew neither the currency used in this country nor the price he should charge for an orange. At the moment, one sailor from the ship joked, "One coin for each." The man that asked for the price took out a coin and handed it to Wen, "Give me one to have a taste." Wen took the money and noticed it was made of silver which weighs around one tael. He was overjoyed and thought, "It cost me one tael of silver to purchase these two baskets of oranges, now I'm earning the money back with only one orange."

The buyer peeled the orange off and a sweet smell was given off right away. "It's such a rarity!" He said while eating, "I want to buy ten more and present them to my master."

Hearing this, nobody could resist the temptation and they all took out their money to buy some Dongting Red. Some bought ten, some bought five... Before long one of the baskets was about to be sold out. Some people were regretting they didn't bring money with them.

Seeing that the oranges would soon be sold out, Wen said immediately, "The remaining are not for sale. I will keep them for myself."

The customers became anxious and said, "How can you stop selling? I'd like to pay four coins for two!"

As the bargaining was going on, there suddenly came a man riding a large horse. He yelled, "Stop selling! I will take all the rest!" Everyone raised their heads and realized it was the person who came first to buy the oranges. He jumped off the horse and ran to Wen, "Hey, orange seller, I will take all the oranges left because my master wants to buy them and present to the king." Hearing that the oranges were to be sent to the king, all others soon stopped scrambling and stood by to see what would happen. Wen, as a clever guy, started thinking, "Since they are for the king, he must be able to pay me more." So he said, "The remaining ones weren't for sale, but if you do want them, please pay three coins for each."

"No problem!" The man didn't bargain at all but said, "Just count them for me." Wen counted the oranges and found there were 52 in total. Then the man paid 156 coins and took the oranges away with much joy.

Wen returned to the ship with the coins he received, and counted them: there was about 1000 coins, equaling 1000 taels of silver. "I didn't expect the two baskets of oranges to be sold for 1000 taels of silver. It only cost me one tael to purchase them. That's incredible!" Wen thought with delight.

The sky went dark and all the crew had come back to their ship. Wen shared his story of selling the oranges with others and the people were all amazed. Someone felt remorseful, "The two baskets of oranges were sold for 1000 taels? If only I also brought some here for sale!" Others congratulated him and said,

"It seems your misfortune has come to an end, and all what awaits you is good luck." Someone else said, "You should use the money you earned to purchase some merchandise here and sell them back in China. This way, you could make even more money." Wen thought for a while and said, "People all call me 'bad luck guy' because I used to lose money for whatever I had sold. But thanks to you guys this time, I earned 1000 taels of silver without any cost. Still, I dare not hope for more money. I'm quite satisfied with what I've made." Hearing his words, people all sighed, "Alas! What a pity to let go the chance to earn more!"

Section 4 Finding the Large Tortoise Shell on the Island

All of the crew members earned a lot of money during their first trip to Chi Ling. Zhang Chengyun said to them, "We had a smooth trade journey this time, and every one of us has made some money. Now the sea looks calm and tranquil, shall we travel farther to earn more?" People all agreed, "Sure! Sure! Let's continue our sea journey!" Thus, the large ship set sail again and was approaching Persia.

One day, a strong wind suddenly began to blow on the peaceful sea and black clouds blotted out the sky: a rainstorm was coming. Worrying that there might be some risks, Zhang immediately told the sailors to anchor the ship at a nearby island. As the ship stopped, heavy rain began to fall. After a while, it became sunny and everybody was relieved. Zhang said, "Let's have a rest here and set off again tomorrow."

Wen felt bored staying on the ship and wanted to visit the island. Others told him, "It seems there are no traces of humans on the island, so it may be dangerous there. You'd better not go." But Wen replied, "Don't worry, I won't walk far."

He walked onto the island and found there were tall trees everywhere, and even the grass had grown to a man's height. There was a small hill which constituted a wonderful scene not far away. Wen thought, "Why not go to the hilltop and enjoy the scenery?" Luckily the hill was not very high and he climbed to the top soon. He looked around the hilltop: everywhere was lush and the view was as beautiful as he anticipated.

All of a sudden, he saw a big creature that resembled a large tortoise nearby. Could there be such a gigantic tortoise? It looked just like a small hill! Wen became anxious right away, "It seems my luck hasn't become better. This huge tortoise will eat me for sure." He intended to turn around and run towards the ship, but feared that the tortoise would chase after him. So he had no other choice but to squat there, observing the horrible, giant creature carefully. After some time, he found the huge tortoise was still motionless. "Could it be a dead tortoise?" Wen tried to get closer to it, and still, the creature wasn't making any movement at all. As he reached the front of it, Wen discovered that it was nothing but a giant tortoise shell. He then heaved a sigh of relief, "It's lucky for me that it's just a shell. Therefore, there must be highly dangerous animals on this island. I'd better return to the ship soon."

Wen turned around and was about to leave. He thought after walking for only a few steps, "Why not bring this huge shell back? My friends may never have seen such a giant tortoise. Later I can also boast in front of my neighbors and let them know about my extraordinary overseas adventures." With this in mind, he dragged the big tortoise shell and headed for the ship.

As he returned on board, people gathered around him and asked, "What's this, Mr. Wen?"

"All of you have purchased a lot of goods, but this is what I got. Look, such a gigantic tortoise shell! You may have never seen this." Wen said with pride.

"Who would buy such a thing? You can never sell it!" They all laughed at him.

Wen didn't care about that, but just used the huge shell as a chest and placed all his belongings in it.

Section 5 The Persian Merchant Marboh

The wind stopped the next day. Zhang Chengyun said to others, "Since all of us have bought some goods, let's set sail for home now." People all agreed and so the large ship began sailing for Quanzhou. The city, at that time, was a bustling port with many businessmen coming and going. Those merchants brought goods to Quanzhou from overseas, which would be purchased by the local businessmen and then sold to various places in the country.

That day, the ship Wen Ruoxu boarded arrived in Quanzhou and the crew started to unload their goods. The only item Wen had was the large tortoise shell, so he was not in a hurry to carry it ashore. At that moment, a man came and said loudly to them, "Fellow merchants, our boss Mr. Marboh is going to treat you to a dinner!"

Wen asked in surprise, "Brother Zhang, who is the guy Marboh?"

Zhang told him, "Marboh is a very famous Persian merchant here in Quanzhou. He is extremely rich and insightful so he can figure out how much your cargo is worth at a glance."

The crew followed the man and arrived at a large restaurant. The sign read 同福饭店, meaning "Sharing Happiness Restaurant". A tall foreign man was standing at the front gate. Zhang Chengyun whispered to Wen, "That is Marboh, people all call him Boss Ma." Wen raised his head and saw the man had blue eyes and a high nose. He had a bushy beard and dressed the same way as the Chinese.

It seemed that many people were quite familiar with Marboh as they were exchanging warm greetings with him. "It was beyond my expectation that this Persian man could speak Chinese so well!" Wen praised him in his heart.

Then Marboh said loudly to the crowd, "To my old and new friends, I am Marboh, a Persian businessman. Today, I'd like to treat you here with wine and dinner. Please show me all the treasures you brought this time, and I shall give you the highest offer." Therefore, people all came over to introduce the goods they had purchased. One said, "Boss Ma, I brought a lot of pearls with me this time…" Another man said, "Boss Ma, I purchased many gemstones this time…" Marboh was overjoyed and invited those merchants with the most treasures to sit at his side.

After a while, he walked to Wen and asked with a smile, "Sir, what treasures do you have?" Having purchased no commodities, Wen didn't know how to reply and felt very embarrassed. Zhang Chengyun came over to help him out, "Boss Ma, this is my friend. He traveled with us just to have some fun." Marboh gave a smile without saying anything, and then turned to the other merchants.

The seating order during the feast was carefully arranged: those who brought more precious items would sit nearer to Marboh; whereas, those who brought lesser goods or commodities with lower values had to sit somewhere in the back. Having no goods with him, Wen Ruoxu was therefore asked to sit in a quiet corner.

Seeing that others were having a jolly time chatting while no one was paying any attention to him, Wen felt a bit sad, "Alas! I earned 1000 taels of silver this time, but it's nothing compared to the wealth of these business giants! If only I also purchased some goods so I wouldn't lose face like I am right now." Watching people chat and drink to their heart's content, he couldn't help but to recall his misfortunes, "Alas! Now that no one notices me, I'll drink by myself." Indulging himself in liquor, Wen became drunk and then fell asleep on his chair.

Section 6 The Tortoise Shell Turned a Treasure

As he woke up the next day, Wen found himself already in bed. He sat up with a headache. No matter how hard he tried, Wen couldn't remember how he returned to the ship last night. Suddenly a noise was heard outside, "Hello, Boss Ma!" "Good morning, Boss Ma!" It turned out Marboh had boarded the ship to check the goods. Everyone was vying to introduce his goods to the rich merchant.

"Boss Ma, these are my gemstones. Please take a look."

"Boss Ma, check out my pearls, please."

Marboh nodded his head politely while looking around the ship. He didn't seem very satisfied with the goods he saw. Before long he reached the side of Wen's "trunk", the tortoise shell and touched it. Then he said excitedly, "Whose item is this? Is it for sale?"

"That belongs to Wen Ruoxu." People all felt strange that

Marboh was interested in the tortoise shell.

"Wen Ruoxu? Was he present at my banquet yesterday?" Marboh didn't have any recollection of that name.

"Yes, of course. He sat at the very back and got drunk in the end. He's now on board." People reminded him.

"My goodness! Excuse me for my poor entertainment of such an honored guest. How could I leave Mr. Wen at the very back? Come on, let me meet again with Mr. Wen." Marboh was eager to see Wen.

People led Marboh to Wen. Marboh made a deep bow to him and said, "Mr. Wen, it was my fault yesterday to offer you such cold treatment. I'm now going to hold another banquet exclusively for you. Please accept my invitation!"

Others were surprised to see Marboh treating Wen so politely. Someone said, "Marboh must be mad! Wen doesn't have any goods except the tortoise shell. Could it be so valuable?" Another person said, "Who knows? People all said this Persian merchant is a knowledgeable buyer, but it seems he's just so-so."

Wen was also surprised to find Marboh, who gave him the cold shoulder the day before, suddenly changed his attitude towards him. He thought, "Since he has offered me the invitation, why not go and see what he wants?" Thus, he followed Marboh to the same restaurant, where a far more sumptuous banquet had already been served. Marboh invited Wen to sit in the middle and accompanied him by the side, while other merchants were all seated at the less important positions.

"Mr. Wen," Marboh raised his cup and said, "Please accept

my sincere apology for my poor treatment yesterday. I've been doing business for more than ten years, and you are the most distinguished guest I have ever met." Saying so, Marboh finished off his wine in a second.

"You flatter me! Actually, I didn't purchase many goods this time. Why are you treating me so well, Boss Ma?" Wen voiced the question in his mind.

"Don't be too modest, Mr. Wen! I've checked your commodity and it is the most valuable item I've seen throughout my business career!" Marboh said while smiling.

"In fact I didn't bring any goods with me. Are you sure, Boss Ma?" Wen felt even more surprised.

"Mr. Wen, aren't you willing to sell it? I mean your treasure, the huge tortoise shell..." Marboh thought Wen didn't want to sell it and so he became a bit anxious.

"Oh, you are referring to the tortoise shell!" Wen finally realized that Marboh had taken a fancy to his big tortoise shell. "Can this tortoise shell be so valuable?" He thought, "But from Marboh's reaction, it could be a treasured item. So I must not let him discern I'm a layman." Therefore, he pretended to be hesitant and said, "I see, Boss Ma, you've taken a fancy to that treasure of mine. In fact, I plan to keep it for myself rather than selling it."

Upon hearing this, Marboh became more anxious and said, "Hey, don't reject me so hastily! At least you can offer a price." Wen was caught in a dilemma because he didn't have any idea how much it was worth. If he valued it too high, Marboh might get angry; if he asked for too little, people would laugh at him. So he turned around and looked at Zhang Chengyun, who secretly showed him five fingers. Wen thought, "5000 taels of silver? Isn't that too much? That's fine, just have a try." So Wen also showed five fingers to Marboh.

"50,000 taels of silver?" Marboh opened his eyes wide and asked.

Wen intended to ask for only 5000, so he didn't expect Marboh would take it as 50,000. He was about to explain, but saw Marboh's eyes were gleaming with excitement. Marboh continued to say, "Are you serious, Mr. Wen? I can pay 50,000 taels to get it?" Wen was perplexed as he wasn't sure whether the price was too high or too low for Marboh. So he just nodded his head.

"Great!" Marboh was so excited that he stood up and said to others, "Let me invite all the friends present to witness that Mr. Wen is willing to sell his treasure to me at the price of 50,000 taels of silver!"

Everyone opened their mouths wide in astonishment. Seeing that Marboh agreed without a second thought to pay such a high price, Wen thought, "I must have asked for too little, but I'm already fortunate enough because no one would ever have anticipated that my tortoise shell would be sold for 50,000 taels. I'm becoming a wealthy person overnight!" He was so delighted that he agreed to sell the treasure to Marboh.

Marboh was worried that Wen would go back on his words. So he said, "Mr. Wen, now that you've decided to sell your treasure to me, please bring it here." Therefore, Wen led a few people on board the ship and brought the giant tortoise shell to the restaurant.

Upon returning, they found Marboh had already prepared several large trunks that contained gleaming silver ingots. He said with a smile, "Mr. Wen, all these silver ingots will be yours. But they're less than 50,000 taels. I also have several houses, the restaurant, and these servants, which altogether amount to the figure. So, they are all yours now!"

Wen was overjoyed to see he had earned so many silver ingots along with houses and a restaurant of his own. So he handed over the tortoise shell to Marboh, who was extremely excited and ordered his servants to carefully put it away.

Having become rich overnight, Wen thought, "Today, I finally had a change in my luck!" He stood up and said to the other businessmen traveling with him, "I used to be a man of bad luck. I lost money in every business transaction I have ever conducted. However, I've reached such a big deal this time. I owe my change in luck to your company and this overseas trip. Therefore, I decided to present each of you with 100 taels of silver. Please kindly accept it! "

Everybody was very glad to receive the silver and they expressed their gratitude to Wen. He then walked to Zhang Chengyun and said, "Brother Zhang, it was beyond my wildest dreams to make such a huge fortune from this trade journey. I owe you a big debt of gratitude. Here is 1000 taels of silver, please accept it as my regard!" Zhang replied, "Well, don't attribute the credits to me! No one is doomed to have bad luck, and since good luck has come, you will make a fortune no matter what business you are engaged in. Congratulations!" With these words, he accepted the silver ingots and thanked Wen.

Section 7 The Secret Behind the Huge Tortoise Shell

Having moved into Marboh's house, Wen Ruoxu couldn't fall asleep the whole night.

The next day, Marboh came to Wen and said, "Mr. Wen, I'm going to return to Persia so I came specially to bid you farewell." Wen asked, "Boss Ma, since you have been in Quanzhou for so many years, what prompted you to make the decision to go back?"

Marboh said with a smile, "All my possessions here have been transferred to you, but thankfully, I have that giant tortoise shell. I will sell it after returning to my country, and by doing so, my sons, my grandsons, and myself would no longer need to work."

Wen said, "Boss Ma, I've been pondering on a question and would like to seek the answer from you: what's so special about that tortoise shell and why is it so valuable?"

Marboh burst into laughter and said, "I know Chinese people worship the dragon, so how come you don't know the tortoise shell?"

"Does the shell have anything to do with the dragon?" Wen felt even more confused.

Marboh explained to him, "Legend has it that each dragon had nine sons while each son had its own looks. Among the children of the dragon, there was one named 鼍龙, or *tuo* dragon. It could live for 10,000 years. This type of dragon was born with a shell which made it look just like a tortoise. It would change its shell every 100 years. When it reached 1000 years old, it would change its shell for the last time, hence becoming a dragon in the true sense and fly away. By this time there would be 24 legendary luminous pearls left in its shell. The pearls were so large that when taken out at night, the whole room would be illuminated by it. The "tortoise shell" you sold to me is actually a shell left by the *tuo* dragon right before it became a real dragon. I already had it opened and indeed found 24 luminous pearls inside. In my country, each of these pearls can be sold for a price as high as 50,000 taels of silver!"

Upon hearing the explanation, Wen opened his eyes wide in amazement. The "tortoise shell" he picked up turned out to be such an invaluable treasure. He was also pleased that he had met the experienced and knowledgeable Marboh, without whom he might still use it as an ordinary trunk.

From then on, Wen Ruoxu settled in Quanzhou and began leading a happy life. Henceforth the story of the "bad luck guy" turning into a wealthy man has been passed on to this day.

练习题 Reading exercises

一、选择题。Choose the correct answer.

1. 下面哪个不是文若虚从小就精通的？（   ）

    A. 画画儿　　B. 下棋　　C. 读书　　D. 做生意

2. 下面哪些倒霉事不是文若虚遇到的？（   ）

    A. 卖扇子赔钱　　　　B. 考试不成功

    C. 卖橘子赔钱　　　　D. 未婚妻去世

3. 文若虚为什么跟张乘运出海？（   ）

    A. 他想去赚钱　　　　B. 他想去散散心

    C. 他想去寻找鼍龙　　D. 他想去买一些货物

4. 关于洞庭红橘子，下面哪句话不正确？（   ）

    A. 洞庭红在中国非常贵　B. 洞庭红会变成红色

    C. 洞庭红非常好吃　　　D. 洞庭红一开始是绿色的

5. 下面哪种情况和小说中不一样？（   ）

    A. 很多人来买文若虚的橘子

    B. 文若虚把橘子都卖给了国王

    C. 橘子很快就卖完了

    D. 文若虚卖橘子赚了很多钱

6. 大船为什么停到了一座岛旁边?（　　）

　　A. 岛上有很多人买东西

　　B. 岛上有很多乌龟

　　C. 遇到了暴风雨

　　D. 岛上有很多橘子

7. 文若虚在岛上发现了什么?（　　）

　　A. 一只大乌龟　　　　B. 一只鼍龙

　　C. 一个大龟壳　　　　D. 很多人

8. 关于玛宝哈,下面哪句不正确?（　　）

　　A. 玛宝哈是波斯人

　　B. 玛宝哈的汉语非常好

　　C. 玛宝哈以前是文若虚的朋友

　　D. 玛宝哈最后回到了波斯

9. 玛宝哈为什么要买文若虚的大龟壳?（　　）

　　A. 龟壳里有夜明珠　　B. 龟壳可以做药材

　　C. 龟壳很少见　　　　D. 龟壳来自波斯

10. 文若虚最后在哪个城市生活?（　　）

　　A. 北京　　B. 泉州　　C. 苏州　　D. 广州

二、判断题：请根据故事内容判断下列说法是否正确，如果正确请标"T"，不正确请标"F"。
Decide whether the following statements are true (T) or false (F).

1. 文若虚小的时候过得很幸福。（　）
2. 文若虚结婚以后不久，妻子就去世了。（　）
3. 文若虚在苏州卖扇子，结果赔了钱。（　）
4. 张乘运是文若虚的好朋友，他常常出海做生意。（　）
5. 文若虚带了十几筐洞庭红去了海外。（　）
6. 文若虚的洞庭红在波斯国卖得很好，赚了不少钱。（　）
7. 文若虚在岛上发现了一个大龟壳，他把它拖到了船上。（　）
8. 玛宝哈第一次见到文若虚，就对他非常客气。（　）
9. 玛宝哈花了五万两银子去买文若虚的大龟壳。（　）
10. 大家都不知道大龟壳的秘密，只有玛宝哈知道。（　）

三、选择填空。 Choose the appropriate words to fill in the parentheses.

1. 文若虚从小就是一个（　　）的孩子，他的父亲是一个商人，家里比较（　　），所以他的童年是（　　）的。长大以后，有人给他介绍了一个（　　）的新娘，但是还没有结婚就（　　）了。文若虚感到自己非常（　　）。

  A. 幸福　　B. 倒霉　　C. 聪明
  D. 富裕　　E. 漂亮　　F. 去世

2. 洞庭红是一种橘子，开始的时候是（　　）的，过一段时间就会变成（　　），这些橘子的（　　）非常好。洞庭红剥开以后，（　　）立刻散发出来。很多人来（　　）买洞庭红，没有买到的人都很（　　）。

  A. 抢着　　B. 味道　　C. 绿色
  D. 红色　　E. 香气　　F. 后悔

3. 文若虚听了朋友的（　　），准备到北京去卖扇子。没想到他到北京的第二天就开始下雨，文若虚（　　）雨赶紧停。但雨停了以后，扇子上的画已经是（　　）的了。文若虚（　　）了一下，只有十几把扇子还可以卖。

  A. 赔本　　B. 建议　　C. 盼着
  D. 期待　　E. 乱七八糟　　F. 收拾

四、请根据故事内容给下列句子排列顺序。
Put the following statements in order according to the story.

A. 他把乌龟壳卖给了玛老板，一下子成了大富翁。

B. 文若虚是个非常聪明的读书人。

C. 文若虚跟随张乘运出海做生意，带了两筐洞庭红橘子。

D. 虽然他很努力，但是考试没有成功，做生意总是赔钱。

E. 橘子红了，很多人都围上来买。

F. 大船停在岛边，文若虚在岛上找到了一个大乌龟壳。

G. 文若虚到了泉州，遇到了一个波斯商人玛宝哈。

五、思考题。Answer the following questions according to the story.

1. 文若虚为什么能转运发财？

2. 玛宝哈是一个怎样的商人？

3. 通过这个故事，你学到了什么？

练习题答案 Keys to the exercises

一、选择题
1. D 2. C 3. B 4. A 5. B
6. C 7. C 8. C 9. A 10. B

二、判断题：请根据故事内容判断下列说法是否正确，如果正确请标"T"，不正确请标"F"
1. T 2. F 3. T 4. T 5. F
6. F 7. T 8. F 9. T 10. T

三、选择填空
1. C D A E F B
2. C D B E A F
3. B E A C E F

四、请根据故事内容给下列句子排列顺序
B-D-C-E-F-G-A

五、思考题
（答案略）

词汇表
Vocabulary List

安慰	v.	ānwèi	console, comfort
岸	n.	àn	shore, bank
摆	v.	bǎi	serve, arrange
宝石	n.	bǎoshí	gem, precious stone
宝物	n.	bǎowù	treasure
笔	m.w.	bǐ	sum
表现	v.	biǎoxiàn	show, manifest
剥	v.	bāo	peel, shell
不知不觉	idiom	bùzhī-bùjué	unknowingly, unconsciously
步	n.	bù	step
财产	n.	cáichǎn	wealth, possession
潮湿	adj.	cháoshī	wet, damp
称赞	v.	chēngzàn	praise, commend
城墙	n.	chéngqiáng	city wall
惩罚	v.	chéngfá	punish
崇拜	v.	chóngbài	worship, admire
出海	v.	chūhǎi	travel overseas
传来	v.	chuánlái	pass, transmit
吹牛	v.	chuīniú	brag, talk big
答应	v.	dāying	agree, consent
打击	n.	dǎjī	blow, hit
大海	n.	dàhǎi	sea
待	v.	dāi	stay
当官	v.	dāngguān	become an official, reach officialdom
岛	n.	dǎo	island
倒霉蛋	n.	dǎoméidàn	bad luck guy
瞪	v.	dèng	open one's eyes wide
递	v.	dì	pass, hand over

蹲	v.	dūn	squat, crouch
多亏	v.	duōkuī	be owing to
发财	v.	fācái	make a fortune
繁华	adj.	fánhuá	bustling, busy
反正	adv.	fǎnzhèng	since, now that
饭店	n.	fàndiàn	restaurant, hotel
纷纷	adv.	fēnfēn	one after another
丰盛	adj.	fēngshèng	sumptuous, rich
风景	n.	fēngjǐng	scenery, view
风平浪静	idiom	fēngpíng-làngjìng	with gentle breeze and fine ripples, calm and tranquil
疯	adj.	fēng	mad, crazy
付	v.	fù	pay
富翁	n.	fùwēng	man of wealth
干脆	adv.	gāncuì	just, simply
尴尬	adj.	gāngà	embarrassed
赶紧	adv.	gǎnjǐn	quickly, immediately
港口	n.	gǎngkǒu	port, harbor
高档	adj.	gāodàng	luxurious, high-grade
告别	v.	gàobié	bid farewell to
功劳	n.	gōngláo	contribution, credit
恭喜	v.	gōngxǐ	congratulate
贵客	n.	guìkè	distinguished guest
国王	n.	guówáng	king
果然	adv.	guǒrán	really, as expected
喊	v.	hǎn	yell
好奇	adj.	hàoqí	curious
胡子	n.	húzi	beard, mustache
糊涂	adj.	hútu	muddled, bewildered
婚礼	n.	hūnlǐ	wedding ceremony
货物	n.	huòwù	goods, commodity
价钱	n.	jiàqian	price
捡	v.	jiǎn	pick up
简直	adv.	jiǎnzhí	simply
见证	v.	jiànzhèng	witness

讲究	n.	jiǎngjiu	attention to detail, careful study
角落	n.	jiǎoluò	corner, remote place
街	n.	jiē	street
精通	v.	jīngtōng	master, be well-versed in
鞠躬	v.	jūgōng	bow
橘子	n.	júzi	orange
巨大	adj.	jùdà	huge, giant
靠近	v.	kàojìn	approach
科举	n.	kējǔ	imperial examination, a civil service examination system in imperial China to select candidates for the state bureaucracy
颗	m.w.	kē	(for things small and roundish)
壳	n.	ké	shell
客商	n.	kèshāng	traveling merchant
筐	n.	kuāng	basket
老板	n.	lǎobǎn	stall owner, boss
理	v.	lǐ	heed, pay attention to
立刻	adv.	lìkè	immediately; right away
两	m.w.	liǎng	tael, a unit of weight for silver and gold in ancient China. According to the Ming Dynasty standard, one tael equals to approximately 37.3 grams.
龙	n.	lóng	dragon
路费	n.	lùfèi	travel expense
绿油油	adj.	lǜyóuyóu	lush green
乱七八糟	idiom	luànqī-bāzāo	in an awful mess
满足	v.	mǎnzú	be satisfied
慢待	v.	màndài	treat a guest inadequately
媒人	n.	méiren	matchmaker
秘密	n.	mìmì	secret
明朝	n.	Míngcháo	Ming Dynasty (1368-1644)
摸	v.	mō	touch, stroke
难怪	adv.	nánguài	no wonder
爬	v.	pá	climb, ascend
盼（着）	v.	pàn(zhe)	look forward to

赔	v.	péi	lose money in business
碰运气		pèng yùnqi	try one's luck
仆人	n.	púrén	servant
奇特	adj.	qítè	peculiar, extraordinary
谦虚	adj.	qiānxū	modest
抢	v.	qiǎng	scramble for
瞧	v.	qiáo	look, see
去世	v.	qùshì	pass away
忍不住		rěnbuzhù	cannot help but
散发	v.	sànfā	distribute, give out
散心	v.	sànxīn	relieve boredom
晒	v.	shài	dry in the sun
山顶	n.	shāndǐng	hilltop, top of a mountain
扇子	n.	shànzi	fan
商人	n.	shāngrén	businessman, merchant
伸	v.	shēn	stretch out one's hand
身边	n.	shēnbiān	one's side
识货	v.	shíhuò	be a knowledgeable buyer
收藏	v.	shōucáng	collect; store up
熟[1]	adj.	shú	ripe, cooked
熟[2]	adj.	shú	familiar
数	v.	shǔ	count
说媒	v.	shuōméi	act as a matchmaker
四处	n.	sìchù	everywhere, all round
松	v.	sōng	relieve, relax
弹琴	v.	tánqín	play the *guqin* or piano
讨价还价	idiom	tǎo jià huán jià	bargain, haggle over the price
特地	adv.	tèdì	specially
偷偷	adv.	tōutōu	stealthily, secretly
拖	v.	tuō	drag, haul
鼍龙	n.	tuólóng	a type of dragon in ancient Chinese mythology, which is also another name of the Chinese alligator
围	v.	wéi	surround, encircle
位置	n.	wèizhi	position, seat

问候	v.	wènhòu	extend greetings to
乌龟	n.	wūguī	tortoise, turtle
乌云密布		wūyún mìbù	cloud over, be clouded
下棋	v.	xiàqí	play chess
嫌	v.	xián	dislike, complain of
箱子	n.	xiāngzi	box, trunk
想法	n.	xiǎngfa	idea, thought
卸	v.	xiè	discharge, unload
心意	n.	xīnyì	regard, kindly feeling
新娘	n.	xīnniáng	bride
宴会	n.	yànhuì	banquet, feast
宴席	n.	yànxí	banquet, feast
夜明珠	n.	yèmíngzhū	legendary luminous pearl
疑问	n.	yíwèn	question
银子	n.	yínzi	silver, a currency by weight in ancient China that took on the form of silver ingot
在意	v.	zàiyì	mind, care about
粘	v.	zhān	stick, glue
招呼	n.	zhāohu	greeting
招牌	n.	zhāopai	signboard, shop sign
珍贵	adj.	zhēnguì	precious, valuable
珍珠	n.	zhēnzhū	pearl
郑重	adj.	zhèngzhòng	serious, earnest
值	v.	zhí	be worth
纸张	n.	zhǐzhāng	paper
主人	n.	zhǔren	master, host
转身	v.	zhuǎnshēn	turn around
转运	v.	zhuǎnyùn	have a turn of luck
装¹	v.	zhuāng	pack, fill
装²	v.	zhuāng	pretend
自从	prep.	zìcóng	ever since
自杀	v.	zìshā	commit suicide
醉	v.	zuì	be drunk
尊贵	adj.	zūnguì	honorable, respected

项目策划：刘小琳　韩　颖
责任编辑：刘小琳
英文编辑：韩芙芸
英文翻译：薛彧威
封面设计：E·T创意工作室

图书在版编目（CIP）数据

倒霉蛋航海奇遇记：汉、英 / 王帅改编 . — 北京：华语教学出版社，2016
（"彩虹桥"汉语分级读物 . 4 级 : 1000 词）
ISBN 978-7-5138-1039-5

Ⅰ . ①倒… Ⅱ . ①王… Ⅲ . ①汉语－对外汉语教学－语言读物 Ⅳ . ① H195.5

中国版本图书馆 CIP 数据核字（2015）第 230077 号

倒霉蛋航海奇遇记
王　帅　改编
*
©华语教学出版社有限责任公司
华语教学出版社有限责任公司出版
（中国北京百万庄大街24号　邮政编码 100037）
电话：(86)10-68320585　68997826
传真：(86)10-68997826　68326333
网址：www.sinolingua.com.cn
电子信箱：hyjx@sinolingua.com.cn
新浪微博地址：http://weibo.com/sinolinguavip
北京京华虎彩印刷有限公司印刷
2016年（32开）第1版
2016年第1版第1次印刷
（汉英）
ISBN 978-7-5138-1039-5
定价：19.00元